YOUR SHAPE, YOUR CLOTHES AND YOU
Secrets of a Successful Wardrobe

Darlene Miller

Illustrations by Andréa L. Brunson
Photographs by Kirk Flynn
Produced by Meerkat Graphics Centre

Darlene Miller
YOUR SHAPE, YOUR CLOTHES AND YOU
Secrets of a Successful Wardrobe
ISBN 0-9642936-0-9

Second Printing

Printed in the United States of America

ACKNOWLEDGEMENTS

I want to extend my sincere thanks to the many people who made this book possible.

To my "research assistants"— Jo, Betty, Eileen, Dede, Janice, Marge, Rhonda, Dianne, Peggie, Karen, Henrietta, Evelyn, Connie, Verna, Ruth, Mary Lou, Sunni, Trudy, Peggy, Jennifer, Pat, Betty Ann, Sheila, Marlene, Myrtle, Sue, Bobbi, Wendy, Beryl, Ruth, Arlene, Jan, Debbie, Vicki, Susan, Kim, and many others. These are the women who have given me great encouragement and given freely of their time to demonstrate the truth of the concepts explained in these pages.

To my illustrator, Andréa L. Brunson, whose talent helps you "see" the concepts I describe.

To my editor, Jamie Kay, for her patience and ability to help me say what I really mean.

To my typesetter, Donna Elliott, for her attractive design.

To my friend, Wendy Norgaard, for her hours of proofreading.

To my hairdresser, Sue Wehmeyer, for making sure every hair was in place.

To models Trudy Khoury, Peggie Pahrman, Deirdre "Dede" White, Rhonda McCarthy, Beth Ikeda, Connie Treichel, Sue Wehmeyer, Deb Rummel, Christy Redler, Liz Redler, Robin Yeager, and Kristie Weatherly, and to photographer, Kirk Flynn, for their willingness to show what real people look like.

To Ireneé Riter for her wonderful interseasonal personal color concept, the Ireneé Color System, and for introducing me to basic wardrobe concepts through color.

And lastly, to the two most important people in my life:
My daughter and best friend, Brenda, for her constant faith and encouragement, and my husband, Russell, for his never-ending patience and support.

TABLE OF CONTENTS

DEDICATED TO YOU

"I accept myself as a bundle of possibilities and
undertake the game of making the most of my best."
Anonymous

This book is written for YOU. Through these pages, I'd like you to realize that you have a wonderful body shape. By selecting the correct clothing, you'll always look beautiful, dress with style, and develop a postive self-image.

Fashion designers create clothes with a certain look for a season. They have some great ideas — if you have that season's body type or if your age is reflected in the current fashions. Does this mean their ideas are right and your clothing needs are wrong?

No! It's just that the fashion designers and you have entirely different needs.

It is my sincere hope this book will help you see yourself in a new way. Deep in my heart, I know we can all be beautiful **if** we stop comparing ourselves to someone else's ideals, understand our body shapes' potential, and learn to present who we **ARE** in the most flattering ways.

Sound intriguing? Let's get to it!

Darlene

INTRODUCTION

FREEDOM

Wouldn't you like to live your life free from

ill-fitting, unbecoming clothes
hiding or camouflaging your body
dressing room despair
thinking you don't measure up to the "ideal"?

This book is designed to do just that — free you from clothing frustrations and show you how to be fashionable and dress with style.

What's the secret?

Clothes create a silhouette for your body. When your body shape and your silhouette are the same, the clothes you wear are flattering.

This book will teach you how to recognize your real body shape and select the correct clothing silhouette. Based on years of experience in design and wardrobe consulting, I **know** there's a beautiful you just waiting to be discovered!

Isn't it exciting?

PURPOSE

This book has been designed to help you add to your wardrobe. Let me assure you that you **won't** have to throw out all your clothes and start all over (panic!). You will keep the clothes you like. You'll discover they're your favorites because they already do exactly what these pages suggest. I'll just show you how to have an even better wardrobe with a minimum investment. Sound impossible? Just wait and see!

The illustrations will teach you how to work with your body shape to select the right clothes or patterns, whether you purchase ready-to-wear from retail stores or catalogs, design your own clothes, or hire a seamstress.

GETTING STARTED

Read the discussion about shapes. Then complete the questionnaire to help you determine **your** body shape. Finally, review the illustrations that show you exactly what clothing will work best for you.

After determining your shape and your best styles, wear the styles for a week or two. Listen to what people say about the "new" you and think about how you feel. It may take a few weeks to get used to the new look. Give yourself an honest try.

Then it's time to add to your existing wardrobe. Please don't do this until you're comfortable with the "new" you. Then add only the clothing that's in your best styles. Don't compromise! You have enough guilt garments hanging in your closet without adding more. It will take a little time and money to get from where you are now to where you want to be. Please be patient. The results will be worth it!

I promise.

UNDERSTANDING SHAPE

The universe is made up of lines —
  straight and curved —
    vertical, horizontal, and angled.

When lines connect, they become shapes —
  triangles — squares — circles — ovals.

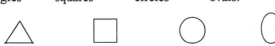

When shapes are combined, additional shapes are formed.

When lines are combined with shapes human bodies are created.

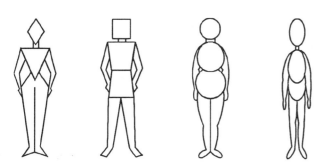

When clothing is placed on body shapes and lines are repeated — a clothing silhouette is created.

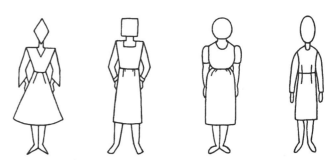

*When the shape of your clothing matches the shape of your body, the effect is **harmony** — a pleasing arrangement of parts.* When you achieve harmony with your wardrobe, the effect is terrific — not just to others but to yourself.

When you recognize your body shape and repeat it in your silhouette, any figure problem you have takes care of itself. That sense of being "together" is far more powerful than whether your hips are larger than your bust. There is so much power in creating harmony, people just don't see or remember imperfections.

Honest!

EXAMPLES OF REAL BODY SHAPES

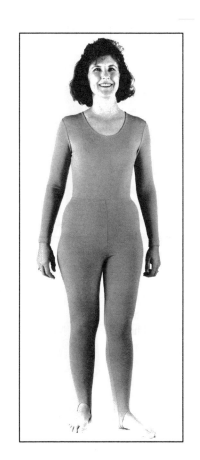

Triangle

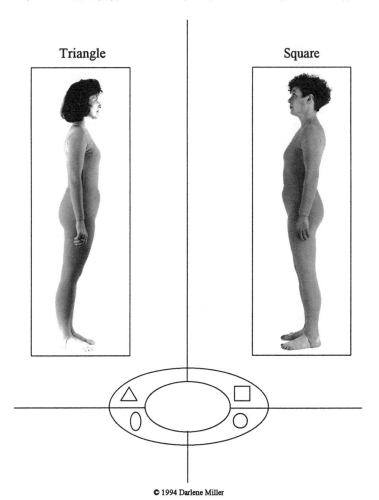

Square

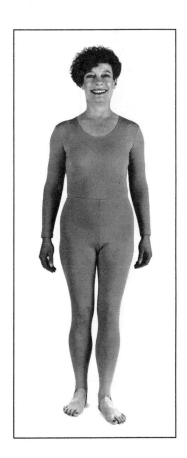

EXAMPLES OF REAL BODY SHAPES

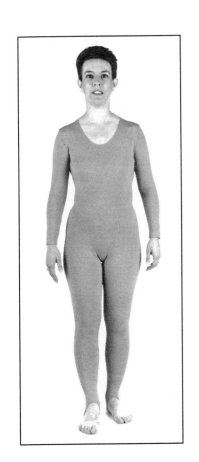

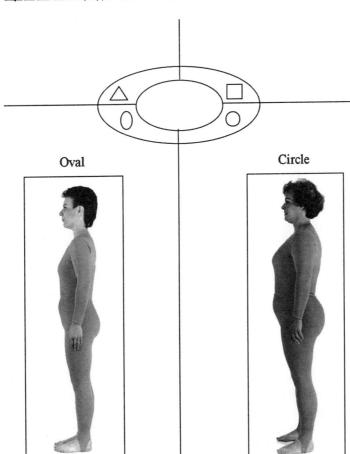

Oval

Circle

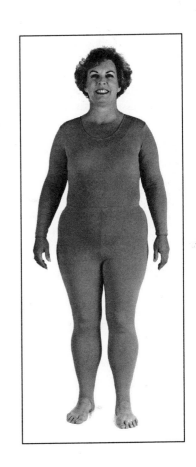

WHAT'S A SILHOUETTE?

Your silhouette is the outline your clothing makes after you're dressed. (Remember doing silhouettes when you were in grade school?) When the shape of your silhouette is the same as your body shape, style is created, and you feel attractive. When your body shape and silhouette don't match, you can feel fat, frumpy, childish, silly, over or under dressed, or just plain uncomfortable.

The most difficult part of learning to dress with style is learning to recognize your silhouette. When you can do that, you won't mix different silhouettes — a common mistake. You won't be tempted to buy clothing on sale just because it's a bargain. Instead, you'll buy what looks good on you. In the end, you'll save money and have a closet full of clothes you wear because you know how good you look in them.

REAL BODY SILHOUETTES

Triangle silhouettes are for triangle bodies. Triangle silhouettes have lines angled in or out from the waist. They accent or exaggerate (such as padded shoulders). They can also have asymmetric or off-balance accents. The look is unusual, often with flare.

Square silhouettes are for square bodies. This silhouette has straight lines up and down, which stabilize and give strength to the outline. Square silhouettes are boxy, squared-off, or stair-stepped. The look is no-nonsense.

Oval silhouettes are for oval bodies. These are body-slimming lines, but they aren't skimpy. This outline has simplicity to it. The shapes of this silhouette are balanced and centered. The look is long and flowing with only slight curves.

Circle silhouettes are for circle bodies. The lines are curved, whether in broad, sweeping circles or S-shapes. The effect is graceful, flowing and feminine. The look is soft and gentle, with a touch of elegance.

CLOTHING DESIGNS FOR SILHOUETTES

The triangle silhouette is extreme. Big shoulders and unusual sleeves, pointed necklines and collars, or other pointed trims and details. The waistline is emphasized by wide belts, fitted or high-rise waists, and peplums. Hip yokes and diagonal darts, pleats, and pockets are featured. Skirts are flared at the bottom, and pants have tapered legs. Unusual jackets and coats can be worn. Novel accessories such as feathers, unique belt buckles, decorative purses, or dramatic leg treatments are good.

The square silhouette has little shaping. Tops with drop shoulders and shirts with collars are emphasized. Sleeves have cuffs and can be pushed up or turned up. Blouson, oversized, dropped, or no-waist styles are best. Pleated skirts with stitched-down pleats and skirts of any length work well. Long jackets are best in boxy, walking, or double-breasted styles. Square, patch pockets and square purses add strength. Practical accessories of leather, wood, ceramic, or natural stones are best.

Oval silhouettes are body slimming. Clothing has smooth shoulders with no shoulder pads. Oval necklines and simple collars go with set-in, long, fitted sleeves. Tops may be leotard-tight. Midriffs and waistlines are fitted and smooth. Darts are straight on narrow skirts and straight leg pants. Medium-length jackets, fitted or with a panel under the arm, work well. Welt pockets are a classic detail. Simple accessories, gems, long, center-knotted scarves, and oval-shaped purses are basic.

The circle silhouette chooses softer styles. Necklines and collars are rounded. Tops are fitted or shirred above a gathered waistline. Princess styles are good. Set-in sleeves can be puffed or tapered with no shoulder pads. Skirts end just below the knee, and pants have tapered legs. Pockets are in the side seams. Jackets are short, fitted, and can be worn over dresses. Accessories are softer, belts and sashes, lace and bows, and rounded purses.

EXAMPLES OF REAL SILHOUETTES

Incorrect

Correct

© 1994 Darlene Miller

Following are examples of how honoring your body shape truly does create a feeling of harmony. True beauty is expressed.

TRIANGLE

Trudy's suit creates the perfect △ silhouette; slightly extended shoulders with shoulder shapes, pointed lapel, nipped in at the waistline with a hint of peplum and a pointed front. The straight, diagonal darted skirt is pegged, smaller at the hemline than at the thigh line. All these features honor her △ body shape, and the effect is a pleasing harmony.

When Trudy wears an ◯ jacket the body skimming effect is boring. The semi-fitted jacket adds width and bulk at one of her best features – her small waistline. The effect of the ◯ suit is a ho-hum look, but her △ suit gives a feeling of pizazz.

EXAMPLES OF REAL SILHOUETTES

SQUARE

Peggie is shown wearing her ☐ silhouette: jacket that hangs straight from the shoulders with just a hint of shoulder shaping to create stability in the shoulder area. The straight jacket with square pockets and notched collar follow the straight lines of her torso. Her straight skirt with waistline tucks give her the boxy, relaxed look so perfect for her ☐ body shape.

When Peggie tries to wear the △ jacket, it seems that she's stuffed into the garment, almost like she is holding her breath. The fitted jacket makes her appear much larger in the hips than she really is. The skirt also makes her look larger.

Correct

Incorrect

11

EXAMPLES OF REAL SILHOUETTES

Incorrect

Correct

OVAL

The classic look shown on Rhonda in her ◯ suit is one of quiet sophistication. The body skimming look honors her ◯ body shape. Sleeves are set-in and tapered. The jacket has darting at the waistline and is best worn buttoned, or it will look like a ☐ jacket. The jacket is worn over a simple darted straight skirt.

This ☐ jacket worn on an ◯ body shape gives Rhonda a casual look . . . at the expense of seeming frumpy.

© 1994 Darlene Miller

EXAMPLES OF REAL SILHOUETTES

CIRCLE

In her ○ suit, Dede is the picture of elegance. The set-in, tapered sleeves cover her large upper arms; the bust darting provides the fullness needed in her upper body. The fitted jacket with tucks at the waistline and a hint of a ruffle fits perfectly over a softly gathered skirt, repeating the roundness of her ○ body shape.

When she wears a ☐ suit, it looks like gravity has gotten the best of her. The pleated skirt has too much fullness, and the straight jacket, even though it fits, adds bulk, weighting her down. Without a waistline, she has little style.

When you honor your body shape,
all your "figure problems"
cease to be of any importance.

Correct

Incorrect

WHICH SHAPE ARE YOU?

Are you curious which body shape you have? Fill out the following 12-part questionnaire. Each section relates to a specific physical characteristic. The drawing below shows which body parts the questionnaire refers to.

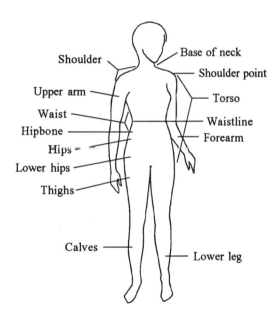

- Shoulder
- Base of neck
- Shoulder point
- Upper arm
- Torso
- Waist
- Waistline
- Hipbone
- Forearm
- Hips
- Lower hips
- Thighs
- Calves
- Lower leg

ANSWERING THE QUESTIONNAIRE

I heartily suggest you take the questionnaire in leotard and tights in front of a full-length mirror. Be honest. No one has to see the answers but you. For some real fun, do the mirror-and-questionnaire game with a good friend. Remember, you really want to hear the truth. The truth will set you free . . . from the chains of ill-fitting, unbecoming clothes.

Before you begin the questionnaire you may want to review pages 4 and 5. In each section of the questionnaire, read the descriptions **carefully** and put a check mark by the information that best describes that area of your body. (And yes, it's O.K. to answer the questions by remembering what you looked like *before* you put on that extra weight.)

- If you can't decide between two descriptions, skip that section; and come back to it later.
- If you really can't decide, check them both.
- And, if it's really difficult, you may want to retake the questionnaire again, several days later.

When you finish, the greatest number of little triangles, squares, circles, or ovals you've checked will be the shape you are. It's perfectly normal not to be consistent throughout your body parts. That's what being human is all about. Please, please remember: don't compare your body to an "ideal" shape. There **is** no ideal shape! **Your** shape is the best . . . because it's YOU.

Are you ready? Let's go!

QUESTIONNAIRE

General Description of Body Shape

△ Body parts appear to look like triangles
Can be broad in both shoulders and lower hips or small in shoulders and large in lower hips and thighs

☐ All body parts fairly straight, very little shape, few curves
Can be long torso with short legs or short torso with long legs

◯ All body parts fairly full and curved
Voluptuous body, roundish
Body is thick from side view
Often appears large boned

◯ All body parts slightly curved, no edges or angles
Good proportion
Graceful, smooth curves
Often smaller in stature

Body Tissue (composition of tissue and fat)

△ Solid muscle tone with exercise
With extra weight tissue becomes soft, flaccid

☐ Solid muscle tone
Muscles remain thin, even with exercise

◯ Firm tissue, with exercise can build body mass, especially in upper body

◯ Average tissue tone
Does not appear muscular or flaccid

Head and Face (head shape may differ from body shape)

△ Pyramid/triangle head on all planes
Wide forehead with pointed chin or narrow forehead with wide jaw or diamond face

☐ Box-shaped or square head, flatish on top
Square face
Square jawline
Possible off-set widow's peak

◯ Ball-shaped head, very round
Head can be large in proportion to rest of body
Round face
Full face

◯ Oval-shaped head, like an egg
Oval on top
Oval face
Possible widow's peak

Neck and Chin

△ Longer neck, sometimes thin — especially in comparison to head
Sharp angle under chin and at base of neck, no fullness
Prominent jaw

☐ Slender neck in comparison to head
Slight fullness under the chin (from jaw to neck)
Sharp angle at base of neck

Neck and Chin (continued)

○ Short and thick neck, similar in width to head
Fullness at back of neck across the shoulders and at base of neck
Fulllness under chin, appearance of double chin

◯ Neck average length and size, proportioned with head
Gradual slope under chin from jaw to neck
Gentle slope at base of neck

Shoulders (natural slope is a 2" drop from base of neck to point of shoulder)

△ Less slope, can be fairly straight across
May be broad or narrow in shoulder width

☐ Less slope with sharp angle at base of neck and at shoulder point

○ Extra muscle at base of neck making shoulders appear sloping
Very rounded at shoulder point

◯ Most slope with smooth angle at base of neck and at shoulder point

Arms

△ Fuller upper arm, tapering into elbow
Fuller forearm, tapering into smaller wrist

☐ Longer, straight arms
Very little shape or difference in size from upper arm to wrist

○ Short arm with fullness at upper outer arm
Full forearm with smaller wrist
Sometimes an indentation on outer arm between shoulder point and full upper arm
Upper arm can be very muscular

◯ Gradual, smooth upper arm and forearm
Well-shaped wrist
Sometimes longer arms

Chest and Breasts

△ Collarbones distinctive, even bony, protruding
Concave chest, less cleavage
Pyramid-shaped breasts; nipples lift
Breast tissue soft, even droopy

☐ Collarbones distinctive, even bony
Concave chest; less cleavage
Small or full breasts
Square-shaped breasts, nipples set lower and downturned
Breast tissue firm

○ Smooth collarbone area; sometimes fleshy
More cleavage
Circular-shaped breasts, fullness continues around under arms
Fleshy across back
Breast tissue firm

◯ Smooth collarbone area
Some cleavage
Oval-shaped breasts
Breast tissue soft, even droopy

Ribcage, Waist, and Hipbones

△ V-shaped ribcage
Hipbones set at waistline
Small waistline in proportion to lower hips
Waistline may scoop down at center back

☐ Straight up and down ribcage
Hipbones high-set at waistline
Very little or no waistline indentation
May be short-waisted
Waistline may scoop down at center back
Flesh at sides or back above waistline

○ Rounded, thick ribcage
Top of hipbone 1½" - 2" lower than waistline
Definite waistline indentation, disappears with weight gain
Waistline sometimes scoops down in center front, especially with weight gain; appears long waisted

◯ Oval ribcage
Top of hipbone 2" lower than waistline
Oval, flowing waist from ribcage to hipbone
Slight, smooth waistline indentation
Waistline sometimes scoops down at center front

Back and Derriere

△ Back is straight
Derriere fuller and angled back or flat and angled down and out toward thighs
Hips tilt forward
Swayback

☐ Back flat and straight
Flat, dropped derriere
Hips tilt forward
Swayback

○ Back fuller
Rounded derriere
Hips tilt toward back
Hips rounded on sides

Backward Hip Tilt   Forward Hip Tilt

◯ Center back tends to be oval-shaped rather than flat from side view
Oval-shaped or dropped derriere
Hips tilt toward back

Thighs, Legs, and Ankles

△ Straighter leg or with more angled shape
Full in thighs
Full in lower leg and ankle
Sometimes full in knee, no indentation

☐ Evenly proportioned legs
Slim legs with not much shape
Can be long and thin or short and stocky

○ Curvy legs
Slim ankles, sometimes large calves
Sometimes smaller in knee
Thigh measurement can be smaller than hips

◯ Long, oval line to legs, gradually shaped
Slim ankles

Hands and Feet

△ Ends of fingers and toes form angles
Fingers can be pointed
First finger digit can be angle shaped
Fingernails are angled

☐ Squared-off hands and feet
Long, straight fingers — no shape
First digit of finger can be cubed-looking
Fingernails are square

○ Ends of fingers and toes are rounder
Rounder palm of hand and ball of foot
First digit of finger can be ball-shaped
Fingernails will be rounder

◯ Ends of fingers and toes are oval-shaped
Fingers longer with smooth shaping
Each digit of fingers slightly shaped
Oval fingernails

Weight

Everyone gains weight all over, but each body shape gains weight in specific areas:

△ Gains weight in outer side of thighs, derriere, ankles, and upper arms
May look wide from front but can be slender-looking from side
Upper chest can gain mass

☐ Gains weight all over, especially through the torso, breast, and ribcage
Appears to have no waist
Legs and arms stay thin and are smaller in proportion to rest of body

○ Gains weight through ribcage and derriere
Shoulder point and hip/leg point stay thin even when upper arm and upper hip rounded out with weight
Gains first in upper hip, derriere, and then above waist

◯ Usually thinner
Gains weight in center of body from under chin down through abdomen
Gains in both front and back — body gets thicker not wider

Number checked:

_____ △ Triangle

_____ ☐ Square

_____ ○ Circle

_____ ◯ Oval

My Body Shape is:_____

FROM BODY SHAPE TO CLOTHING

You have just determined you have a _____ body shape. Now, let's see what clothing you will wear.

On the following pages are detailed illustrations of apparel and the terminology used to describe it.

Sometimes the terminology refers to a garment part; sometimes it refers to the whole garment. You need to be able to separate and analyze the parts as well as the whole. That way, you can be sure an entire outfit manifests only one silhouette.

Each page is divided into four sections, one for each body shape. In each section, you'll find the garments best suited for that person's figure.

If it appears that some body shapes have more clothes to wear, remember **each shape has only ONE silhouette.** Sometimes a silhouette has a few more variations. Some of you may ask, "why can't I wear a garment from another section?" Clothing that appears in your section represents your very best options, but these clothes are not the only ones you can wear; they are just the best.

OK so far?

  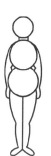    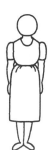 

CLOTHING ILLUSTRATIONS FOR BODY SHAPES

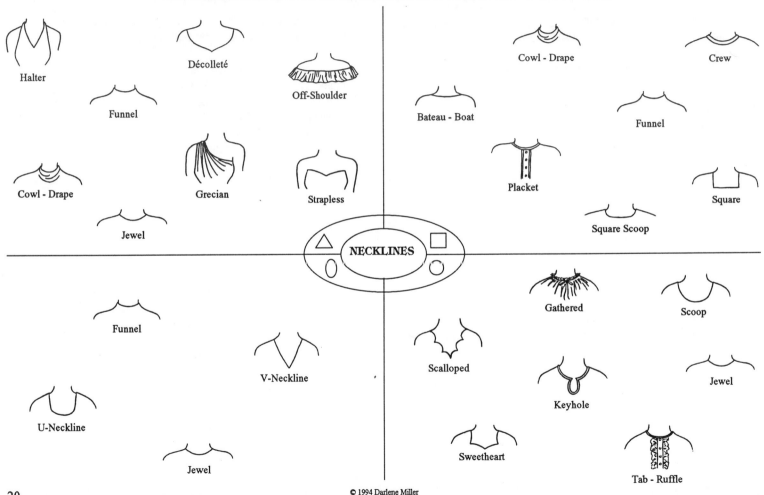

Halter

Décolleté

Off-Shoulder

Funnel

Cowl - Drape

Grecian

Strapless

Jewel

Cowl - Drape

Crew

Bateau - Boat

Funnel

Placket

Square

Square Scoop

NECKLINES

Gathered

Scoop

Funnel

Scalloped

Jewel

V-Neckline

Keyhole

U-Neckline

Jewel

Sweetheart

Tab - Ruffle

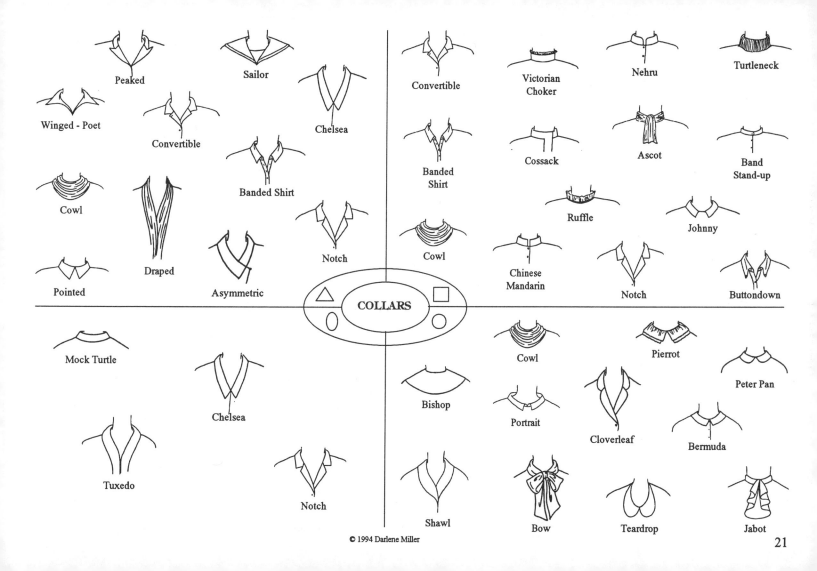

Peaked

Sailor

Convertible

Victorian Choker

Nehru

Turtleneck

Winged - Poet

Convertible

Chelsea

Banded Shirt

Cossack

Ascot

Band Stand-up

Cowl

Draped

Banded Shirt

Convertible

Ruffle

Johnny

Pointed

Asymmetric

Notch

Cowl

Chinese Mandarin

Notch

Buttondown

COLLARS

Mock Turtle

Cowl

Pierrot

Peter Pan

Chelsea

Bishop

Portrait

Cloverleaf

Bermuda

Tuxedo

Notch

Shawl

Bow

Teardrop

Jabot

© 1994 Darlene Miller

21

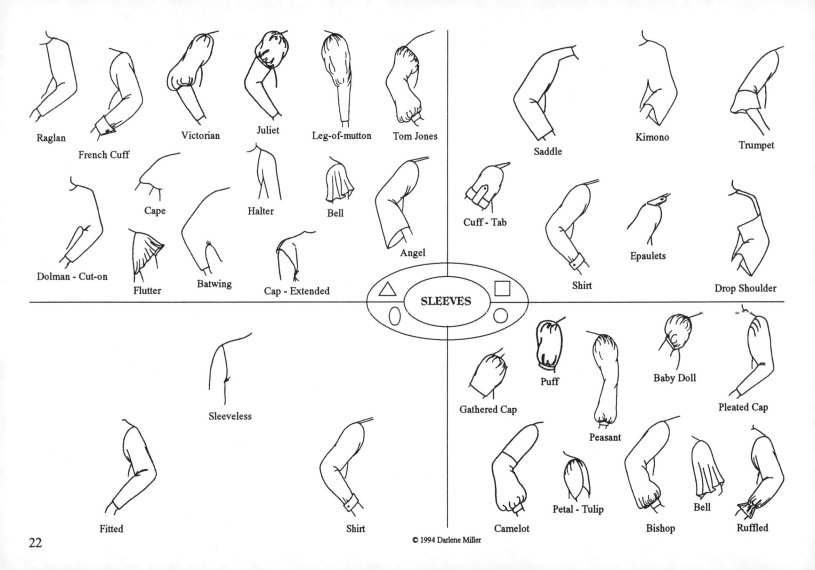

Raglan

French Cuff

Victorian

Juliet

Leg-of-mutton

Tom Jones

Saddle

Kimono

Trumpet

Cape

Halter

Bell

Cuff - Tab

Epaulets

Dolman - Cut-on

Flutter

Batwing

Cap - Extended

Angel

Shirt

Drop Shoulder

SLEEVES

Sleeveless

Fitted

Shirt

Gathered Cap

Puff

Peasant

Baby Doll

Pleated Cap

Camelot

Petal - Tulip

Bishop

Bell

Ruffled

22

© 1994 Darlene Miller

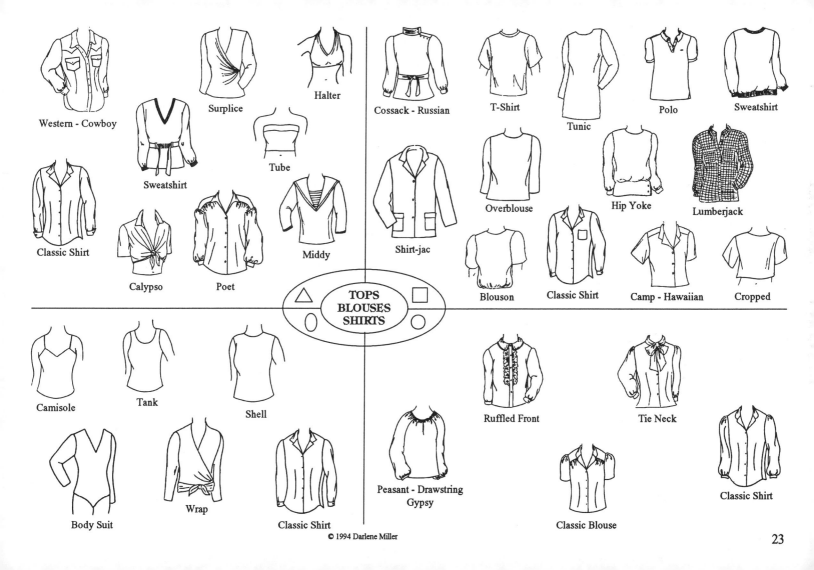

Western - Cowboy

Surplice

Halter

Cossack - Russian

T-Shirt

Tunic

Polo

Sweatshirt

Classic Shirt

Sweatshirt

Tube

Middy

Overblouse

Hip Yoke

Lumberjack

Calypso

Poet

Shirt-jac

Blouson

Classic Shirt

Camp - Hawaiian

Cropped

**TOPS
BLOUSES
SHIRTS**

Camisole

Tank

Shell

Ruffled Front

Tie Neck

Body Suit

Wrap

Classic Shirt

Peasant - Drawstring
Gypsy

Classic Blouse

Classic Shirt

© 1994 Darlene Miller

23

Fanny

Wraparound

Batwing Crossover

Cardigan

Skimp

Fair Isle

Fisherman

Pullover

V-Neck
Cardigan

Crew

Tennis

Cardigan

Poor Boy

Shrink

Pullover

Short Cardigan

SWEATERS

24

© 1994 Darlene Miller

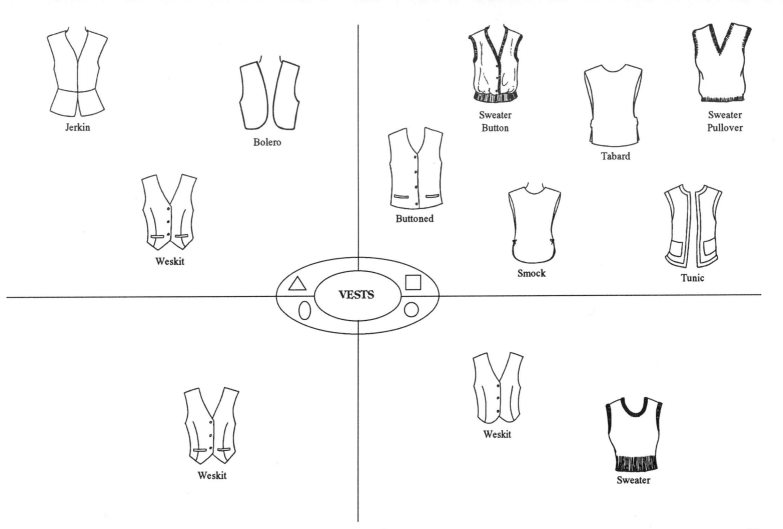

Jerkin

Bolero

Weskit

Sweater
Button

Tabard

Sweater
Pullover

Buttoned

Smock

Tunic

VESTS

Weskit

Weskit

Sweater

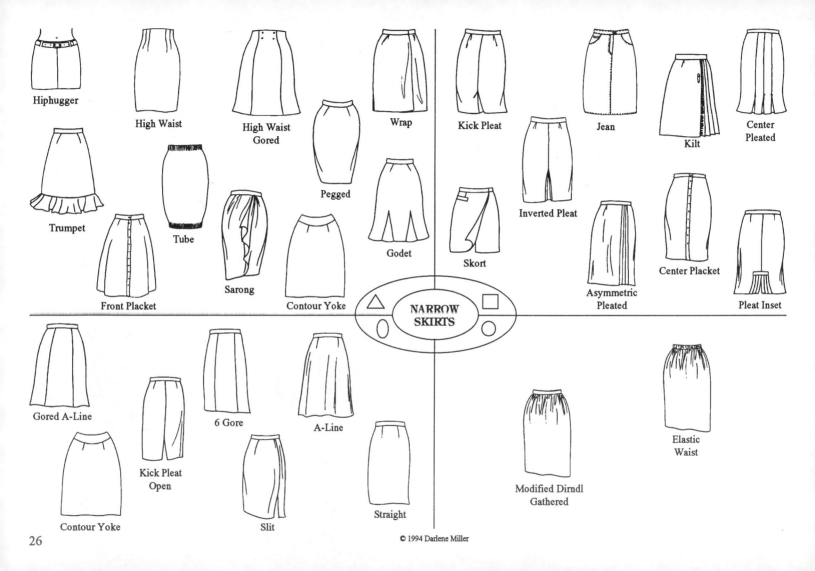

Hiphugger

High Waist

High Waist
Gored

Wrap

Kick Pleat

Jean

Kilt

Center
Pleated

Trumpet

Front Placket

Tube

Sarong

Pegged

Godet

Contour Yoke

Skort

Inverted Pleat

Asymmetric
Pleated

Center Placket

Pleat Inset

NARROW
SKIRTS

Gored A-Line

Contour Yoke

Kick Pleat
Open

6 Gore

Slit

A-Line

Straight

Modified Dirndl
Gathered

Elastic
Waist

26

© 1994 Darlene Miller

Harem

Squaw
Broomstick

Flared

Accordian - Sunburst

Circle

Box Pleat

Knife Pleated

Gored

Fitted Yoke

Bell

Handkerchief

Stitched Down
Pleats

Split - Culottes
Divided - Pantskirt

FLARE
SKIRTS

Gathered Flare

Tiered

Dirndl
Bouffant

Prairie - Peasant - Granny

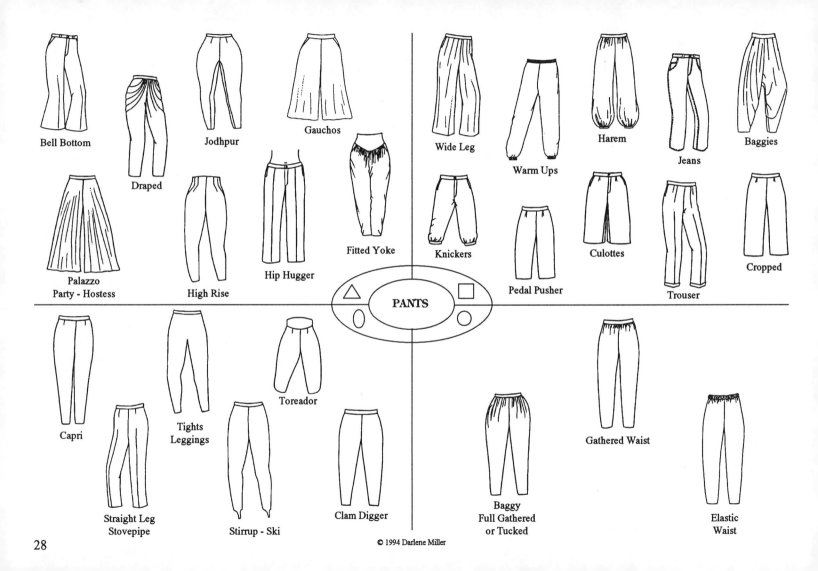

Bell Bottom

Draped

Jodhpur

Gauchos

Palazzo
Party - Hostess

High Rise

Hip Hugger

Fitted Yoke

Wide Leg

Warm Ups

Harem

Jeans

Baggies

Knickers

Pedal Pusher

Culottes

Trouser

Cropped

PANTS

Capri

Tights
Leggings

Toreador

Straight Leg
Stovepipe

Stirrup - Ski

Clam Digger

Baggy
Full Gathered
or Tucked

Gathered Waist

Elastic
Waist

28

© 1994 Darlene Miller

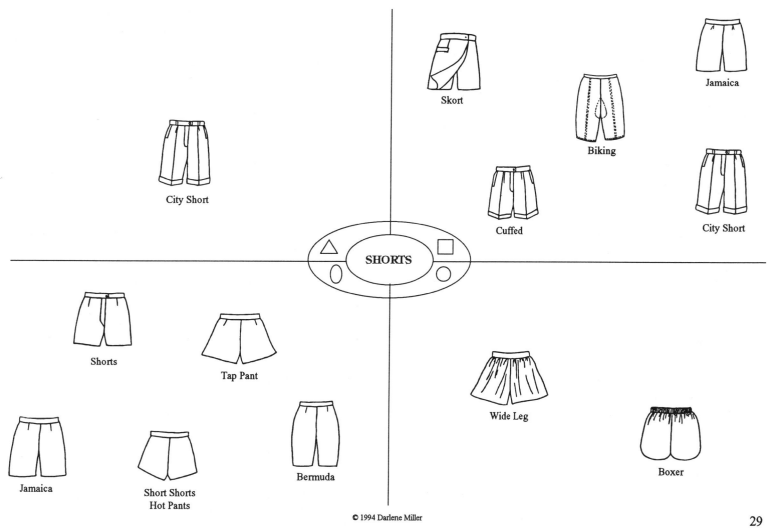

Skort

Biking

Jamaica

City Short

Cuffed

City Short

SHORTS

Shorts

Tap Pant

Wide Leg

Jamaica

Short Shorts
Hot Pants

Bermuda

Boxer

Bouffant

Peplum

Strapless Bustier

Flapper

Fanny Tie - Wrap

Shift - Sweater
Chemise - Sack

Coat Dress

Dropped
Waist

Shirtdress

Peasant
Square Dance

Halter

Tent - Trapeze

Overblouse

Shirtwaist

Float

Blouson

Two-Piece
Blouson

Jumper

△ ◻
DRESSES
◯ ◯

Wrap

Sheath

Princess
A-Line

Slip
Dress

Empire

Midriff

Sundress

Muumuu

Basic - Fitted

Strapless Bustier

Chinese
Cheongsam

Prairie - Granny

Babydoll Smock

Elastic Waist

Pinafore

© 1994 Darlene Miller

30

Bathrobe

Kimono

Teddy

Lounging Pajamas

Negligee

Caftan

Pajama

LOUNGEWEAR

Ski Pajamas

T-Shirt

Nightshirt

Housecoat

Nightgown

Romper

Peignoir Set

Baby Doll

Granny Gown

Teddy

Hostess Coat

Juliet Gown

Teddy

Granny Robe

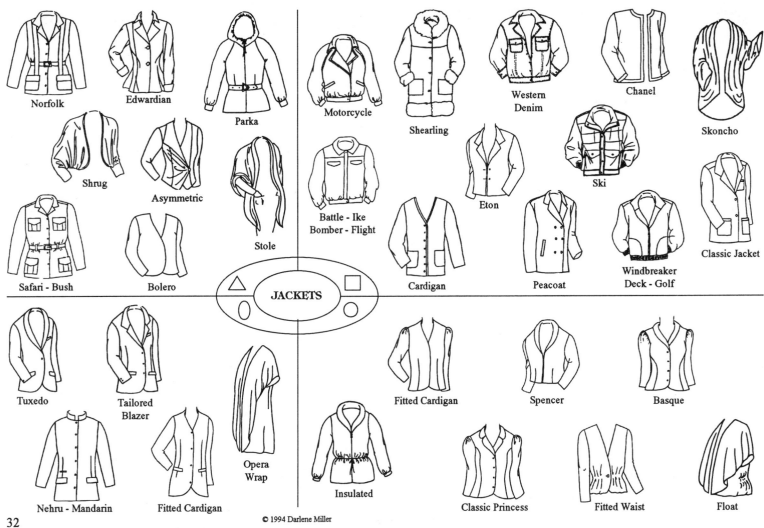

Norfolk

Edwardian

Parka

Motorcycle

Shearling

Western Denim

Chanel

Skoncho

Shrug

Asymmetric

Stole

Battle - Ike
Bomber - Flight

Eton

Ski

Safari - Bush

Bolero

△ ○ JACKETS □ ○

Cardigan

Peacoat

Windbreaker
Deck - Golf

Classic Jacket

Tuxedo

Tailored
Blazer

Opera
Wrap

Fitted Cardigan

Spencer

Basque

Nehru - Mandarin

Fitted Cardigan

Insulated

Classic Princess

Fitted Waist

Float

32

© 1994 Darlene Miller

Coachman

Swagger

Iverness

Carcoat Topper

Admiral

Balmacaan

Duster

Trench
Raincoat

Poncho

Quilted - Down
Storm

Slicker - Duffel
Toggle - Stadium

Cape

COATS

Chesterfield

Classic

Clutch - Wrap

Princess

Polo

© 1994 Darlene Miller

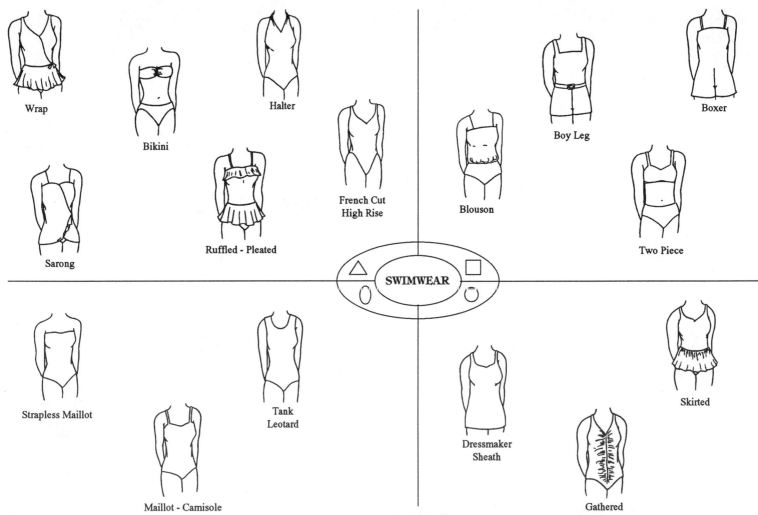

Wrap

Bikini

Halter

French Cut
High Rise

Boy Leg

Boxer

Sarong

Ruffled - Pleated

Blouson

Two Piece

SWIMWEAR

Strapless Maillot

Tank
Leotard

Dressmaker
Sheath

Skirted

Maillot - Camisole

Gathered

34

© 1994 Darlene Miller

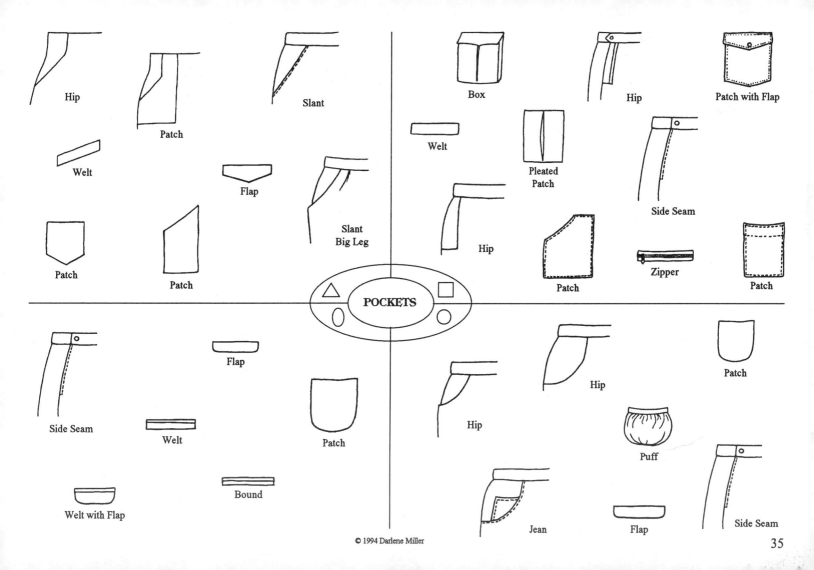

Hip

Patch

Welt

Flap

Patch

Patch

Slant

Slant
Big Leg

Box

Welt

Pleated
Patch

Hip

Patch

Hip

Patch

Zipper

Hip

Patch with Flap

Side Seam

Patch

Side Seam

Welt

Flap

Patch

Hip

Hip

Patch

Puff

Welt with Flap

Bound

Jean

Flap

Side Seam

POCKETS

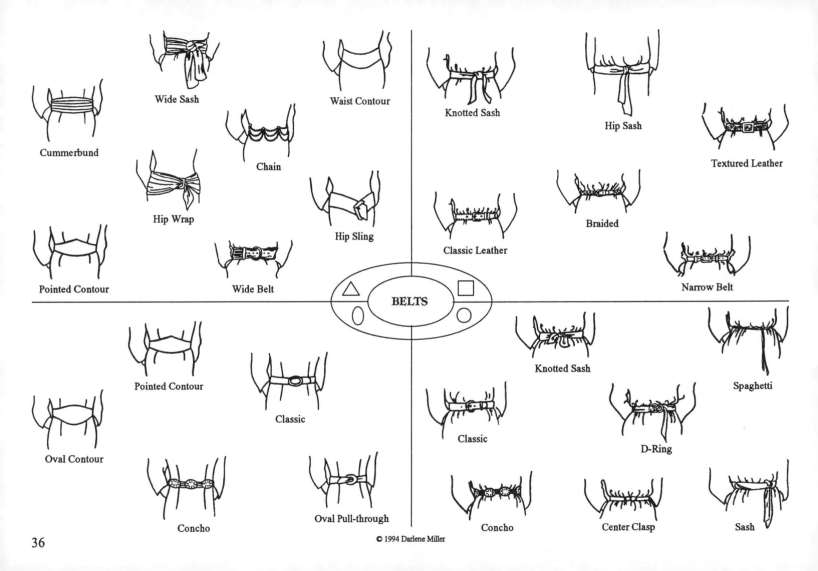

Cummerbund

Wide Sash

Waist Contour

Knotted Sash

Hip Sash

Textured Leather

Chain

Hip Wrap

Hip Sling

Classic Leather

Braided

Pointed Contour

Wide Belt

BELTS

Narrow Belt

Pointed Contour

Classic

Knotted Sash

Spaghetti

Oval Contour

Classic

D-Ring

Concho

Oval Pull-through

Concho

Center Clasp

Sash

36

© 1994 Darlene Miller

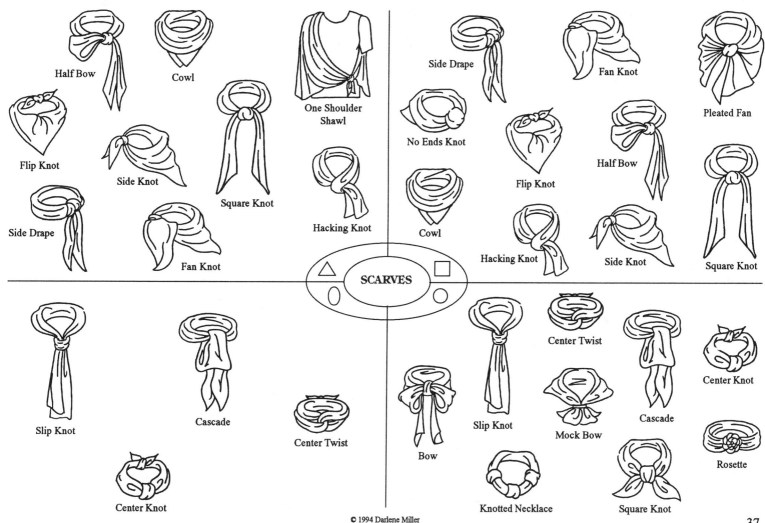

Half Bow

Cowl

One Shoulder Shawl

Side Drape

Fan Knot

Pleated Fan

Flip Knot

No Ends Knot

Side Knot

Square Knot

Flip Knot

Half Bow

Side Drape

Fan Knot

Hacking Knot

Cowl

Hacking Knot

Side Knot

Square Knot

SCARVES

Slip Knot

Cascade

Center Twist

Center Knot

Bow

Slip Knot

Center Twist

Mock Bow

Cascade

Center Knot

Knotted Necklace

Square Knot

Rosette

Cowboy

Huarache

Kiltie

Gladiator

Slide

Ankle Strap

Pump

Dress

Sneaker

Walking

Thong

Clog

Sneaker

Kiltie

Moccasin

Huarache

Saddle Oxford

Dress

Walking - Casual

Mary Jane

Loafer

Mamma

Walking

Espadrille

Pump

T-Strap

Sabot-strap

Casual

Sneaker

Flat - Ballet Ballerina

Sandal

Wedgie

Pump

Sandal

Pump

Wedgie

Open-toe

Thong

Spectator

Walking

Ankle

Flat - Ballet - Ballerina

Sneaker

Thong

Walking

Sandal Pump

Slingback

Dress

Dress

△ ○ SHOES BOOTS □ ○

38

© 1994 Darlene Miller

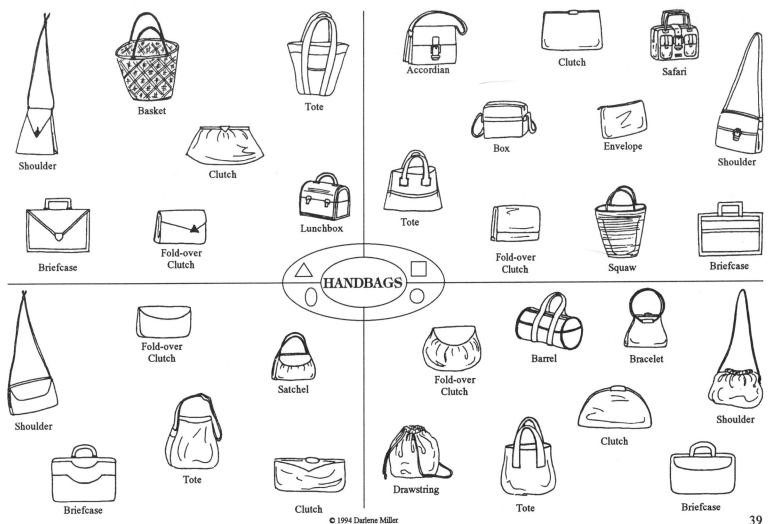

Shoulder

Basket

Tote

Accordian

Clutch

Safari

Clutch

Box

Envelope

Shoulder

Briefcase

Fold-over Clutch

Lunchbox

Tote

Fold-over Clutch

Squaw

Briefcase

△ ☐
HANDBAGS
◯

Shoulder

Fold-over Clutch

Satchel

Fold-over Clutch

Barrel

Bracelet

Shoulder

Briefcase

Tote

Clutch

Drawstring

Tote

Clutch

Briefcase

© 1994 Darlene Miller

39

STYLES THAT WORK FOR ME

Before continuing, take a few minutes to think about the illustrations you've just looked at. Take a moment to jot down the styles that will work for you and the ones you are going to try.

STYLES THAT WORK	STYLES I NEED TO TRY

WHAT TO DO NEXT

Now that you know your **body shape**, silhouette, and the garments which work best for you, how do you **show** what you know?

As I suggested, think of the parts as well as the whole. Look at your blouses, shirts, sweaters, or jackets. Examine necklines, collars, shoulders, sleeves, and waistlines. Do the darts, tucks, gathers, pockets, buttons, and style details repeat your body shape? Examine your skirts and pants the same way. Are you wearing a square sweater with a circle skirt?

Next look at your dresses and jumpsuits. Could a jacket make a suit out of some of them? Sometimes adding the right jacket will create the right silhouette.

Finally, look at your accessories. Do you have the best ones for your body shape? Accessories (shoes, handbags, belts, sunglasses, scarves, and luggage) complete an outfit. They are the little details that add pizazz. They say, ''Hey, I know what I'm doing!''

Use the drawings and photos on the following pages when you go through your closet. They will show you how to analyze ready-to-wear before you take it home and find out it doesn't really work. Also, use these illustrations and photos to help you evaluate patterns and catalog purchases.

Simple, huh?

Are you aware you are about to become a clothing ''designer''? This is exactly what they do – create garments by putting all the parts together. But, your creations will be better – they will fit **your** body!

TRIANGLE

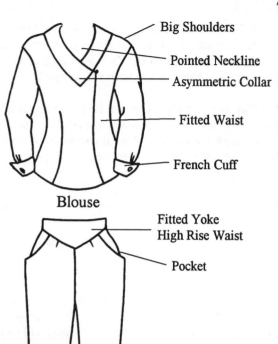

Blouse

- Big Shoulders
- Pointed Neckline
- Asymmetric Collar
- Fitted Waist
- French Cuff

- Fitted Yoke High Rise Waist
- Pocket
- Tapered Leg

Pants

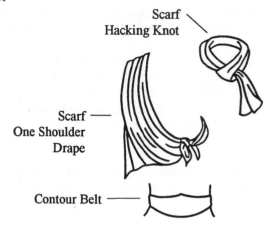

- Scarf Hacking Knot
- Scarf One Shoulder Drape
- Contour Belt

Accessories

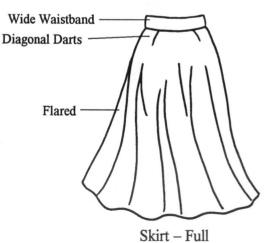

- Wide Waistband
- Diagonal Darts
- Flared

Skirt – Full

TRIANGLE

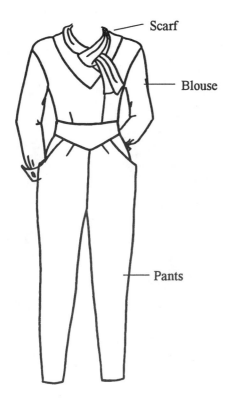

Scarf

Blouse

Pants

Jumpsuit

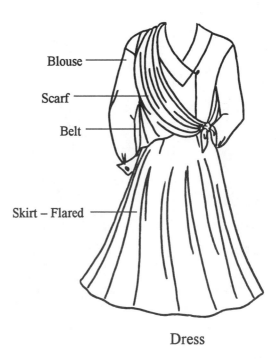

Blouse

Scarf

Belt

Skirt – Flared

Dress

TRIANGLE

Incorrect

Padded shoulders, defined waistline, and full flared skirt are always good on a △. Why would Trudy want to hide in a comfortable tunic that just adds pounds?

44

Correct

Correct

Incorrect

The same is true for Beth, a △, in a cut-on sleeve top, flare skirt, and contrast belt for emphasis. In the dropped waist jumper, she looks somewhat dowdy.

TRIANGLE

Incorrect

Beth in jodhpurs and batwing top, a pizazzy look for a △. Straight legged, pleated jeans with an over sized belt make her look top heavy.

Correct

Correct

Incorrect

For a △ like Trudy, fitted waistline pants with a yoke ending at hipline pockets create the perfect silhouette. The baggy pants and big tunic are overpowering.

SQUARE

Shirt Collar with Band

Drop Shoulder

Square Pocket

Shirt Sleeve

Classic Shirt

Banded Front

Blouse

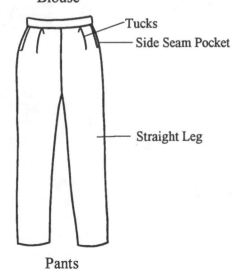

Tucks

Side Seam Pocket

Straight Leg

Pants

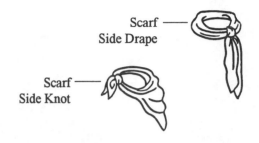

Scarf Side Drape

Scarf Side Knot

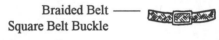

Braided Belt
Square Belt Buckle

Accessories

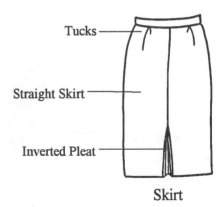

Tucks

Straight Skirt

Inverted Pleat

Skirt

SQUARE

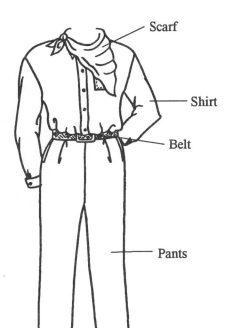

Scarf

Shirt

Belt

Pants

Jumpsuit

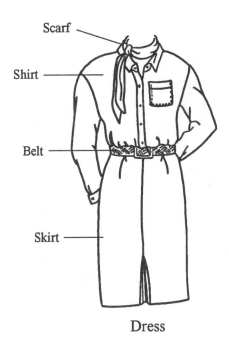

Scarf

Shirt

Belt

Skirt

Dress

SQUARE

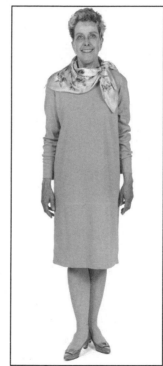

Incorrect

Peggie, a □, looks best in her shirtwaist dress with lots of detail. The △dress leaves her looking unfinished, only half done with her dressing.

Correct

Correct

Incorrect

Why not look tall and slim like □ Connie in a comfortable sack dress? Placing emphasis at the waistline with a △ flare skirt makes her look hippy and short-legged.

SQUARE

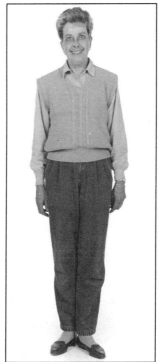

Incorrect

The comfortable tunic is perfect for ☐ Peggie. A fitted yoke with pockets only creates an imbalance for a ☐ shape. For a very different look see Trudy on page 45.

Correct

Correct

Incorrect

Vests are a favorite for ☐ s like Connie. They are comfortable when worn over jeans. An oversized, rounded sweater with flare skort give her the teddy bear look.

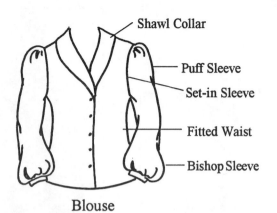

Shawl Collar

Puff Sleeve

Set-in Sleeve

Fitted Waist

Bishop Sleeve

Blouse

CIRCLE

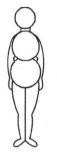

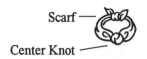

Scarf

Center Knot

Classic Belt
Round Buckle

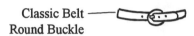

Accessories

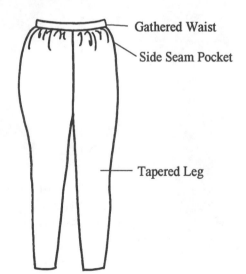

Gathered Waist

Side Seam Pocket

Tapered Leg

Pants

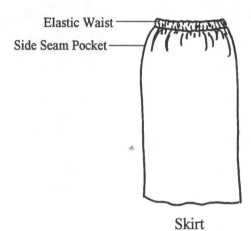

Elastic Waist

Side Seam Pocket

Skirt

CIRCLE

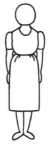

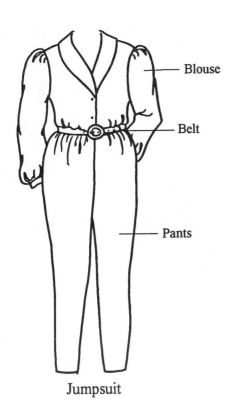

Blouse

Belt

Pants

Jumpsuit

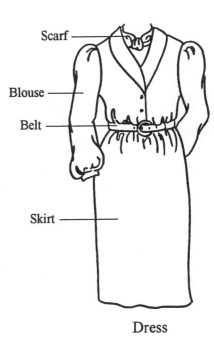

Scarf

Blouse

Belt

Skirt

Dress

CIRCLE

Incorrect

Os like Dede may have a difficult time finding clothing. However, with the correct silhouette, they will have a perky, rather than matronly, look.

Correct

Correct

Incorrect

Sue, a ○, has an innocent look wearing her new dress with fitted bodice, puffy sleeves, and gathered skirt. The dropped waist is definitely a frumpy look.

CIRCLE

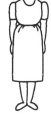

Incorrect

Here Sue, a ◯, looks soft and approachable in clothing that softly flows over her ◯ body shape. Why would she want to look and feel uncomfortable, stuffy, and stiff?

Correct

Correct

Incorrect

Dede looks smashing in a pants outfit – when it repeats her ◯ body shape. What a difference tucking in a top can make, especially with a beautiful scarf at the neckline.

OVAL

Blouse

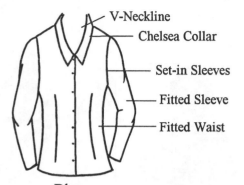

- V-Neckline
- Chelsea Collar
- Set-in Sleeves
- Fitted Sleeve
- Fitted Waist

Blouse

Pants

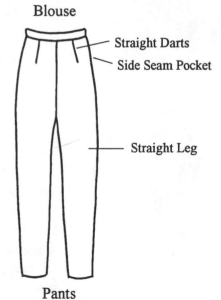

- Straight Darts
- Side Seam Pocket
- Straight Leg

Pants

Accessories

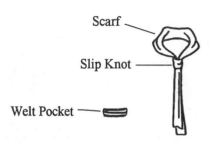

- Scarf
- Slip Knot
- Welt Pocket
- Classic Belt Oval Buckle

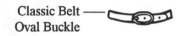

Accessories

Skirt

- Straight Darts
- Side Seam Pockets
- Straight Skirt

Skirt

OVAL

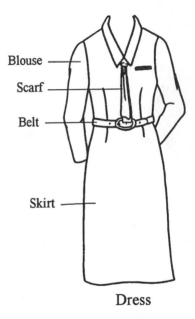

Blouse

Belt

Pants

Jumpsuit

Blouse

Scarf

Belt

Skirt

Dress

OVAL

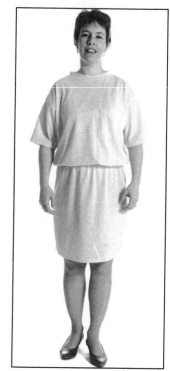

Incorrect

Os can look overwhelmed so easily, like Deb in a dress perfect for a △. The ○ dress is simple, yet so elegant. It's always a dressy look.

Correct

Correct

Incorrect

Put an ○ like Rhonda in a Cheongsam dress for a classic, timeless look. A blouson, drop-shoulder dress makes her look droopy and tired.

56

OVAL

Incorrect

Want to gain weight? Put ○ Rhonda in gathered pants with a loose fitted midriff rather than body-skimming jeans and classic fitted top.

Correct

Correct

Incorrect

A truly sophisticated look – a classic fitted blazer and straight skirt, so right for an ○. Deb appears lost in her □ jacket and △ skirt.

AT ANY AGE

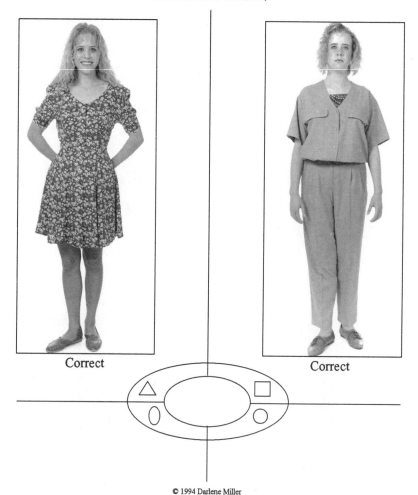

Incorrect

The bouffant dress with the large sleeves, fitted wiast, and flare skirt are right for Christy while the sack dress does not show off her △ body shape.

Correct

Correct

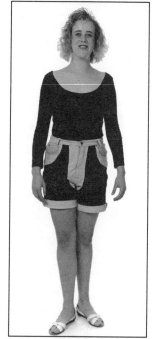

Incorrect

Liz, a □ is great in her casual silk sport outfit with the blouson top and pleated pants. The short outfit makes her look large in the hips.

AT ANY AGE

Incorrect

Subtle sophistication, the look of an ◯. The sheath dress is perfect for Kristie while the short dress with baggy skirt droops at the shoulders and everywhere else.

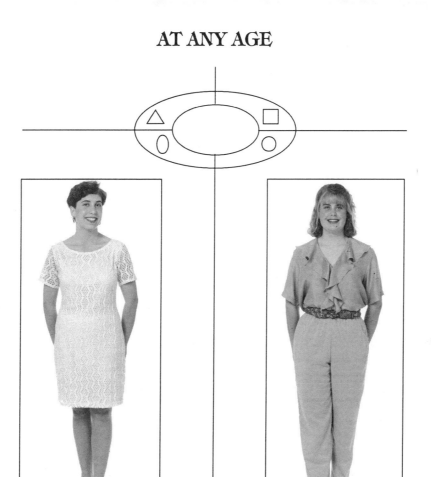

Correct

Correct

Incorrect

◯ Robin, so slim appearing in the ruffled blouse and gathered waist, tapered leg pants while overwhelmed by the loose fitting tunic top and cuffed jeans.

59

HELP! I'M LOST IN MY CLOSET!

Does your closet resemble an Amazonian jungle? Could you get lost in it? Well, you know what to do with chaos . . . straighten it out!

Here's how.

Take everything out of your closet and dresser. As you remove each item, put it into one of three piles:

1) favorites you wear constantly
2) clothes you wear but don't really like
3) clothes you like but don't wear

You'll discover your favorites are your favorites because you look good in them, and there are some beautiful clothes you don't wear because they're either too small, too large, or their silhouette isn't right for you.

Try not to get emotional during this process. Guilt doesn't solve anything. The past is the past, and when it comes to clothes, the past isn't important. From now on, it's the future that's important!

The clothes in Pile Number One will go back in your closet or dresser. Before you put them away, you might want to make sure they are clean and in good repair.

When you put clothes back in your closet, try hanging like garments together and like colors together. If you hang complete outfits together, you may limit your creativity.

Analyze the clothes in Pile Number Two. Ask yourself why you don't really like the piece. Does it fit properly? Is there something that bothers you about the fabric or the color? Does it fit your image of who you are? If the item fits, if you like the fabric and color, and if it works with your life style, it may be time to evaluate it according to your newly-discovered silhouette.

If the garment isn't in your silhouette, read the section entitled, ''Freedom – At Last.'' If you can't or don't feel like solving the problem, put the garment in Pile Number Three.

Box up the items in Pile Number Three. These clothes are ready to recycle. You can give them to friends who have that size and silhouette, sell them at a garage sale, take them to the consignment shop, or give them to a charitable organization.

There, how's that for a fresh start?

FREEDOM – AT LAST

"Style is the ability of a woman to combine her clothing. It's not about spending a lot of money; it's not wearing designer clothes. It's finding what's best for you."

Carol Little

After using this book you will realize some clothing does not work because it combines two or more silhouettes. If you've determined that's a problem, ask yourself if you can add or subtract something to make it work. The secret is to create a look as near to a single silhouette as possible.

WORKING WITH WHAT YOU'VE GOT

Here are ways of changing a silhouette –

Shorten or lengthen skirts or pants. Taper the legs if they're too wide. Add or change a belt.

Look at the sleeves. Are they the right length? Could you turn under the cuffs? Can you roll up the sleeves? Could you take in a sleeve that's too full?

How do the shoulders look? Can you remove or add shoulder pads?

Collars have many options. You can turn some under to create a plain neckline. You can wear jewelry or a scarf to change the appearance. You can wear another blouse or shirt over or under the piece.

You can shorten a too-long jacket.

How about changing the buttons? Could you add larger or smaller ones? A different color? Wooden ones? Unusual shapes?

You'll also be able to change the silhouette by creating new combinations. If your skirts or pants aren't perfect for your silhouette, you may be able to use a different blouse to create the effect you're after. A sweater or vest can do the same job. How about using that not-quite-right blouse under the perfect jacket? If you treat what you have as separates, rather than outfits, you'll have a lot more options than you thought possible.

As you study the photos on the following pages the suggestions for making a garment work for you are not specific to any one body shape. They are suggestions intended to give you alternatives, ideas, and inspiration for changing the garments hanging in your closet. It is important during this time of transition in developing your silhouette to make as many of the things you already have work for you. It will save you money, it will force you to be creative, and besides – it is fun! Once you start you'll be amazed at what you already have, right there, hanging in your closet.

WORKING WITH WHAT YOU'VE GOT

Unattractive

Attractive

Attractive

Unattractive

Create pizazz by changing a belt. Add a nice leather belt, in a contrasting color or a blend. Anyone can wear the belt that comes with the dress. It takes a little thought, effort and a sense of style to put a belt on that works for you.

Trudy is wearing her dress the way it was shown in the store – casual and comfortable. But, on her it looks boring. By tucking in the top and adding a belt, her outfit looks finished, has interest, and still is casual and comfortable.

WORKING WITH WHAT YOU'VE GOT

Unattractive

Attractive

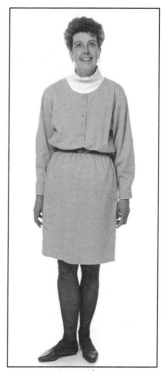

Attractive

Unattractive

Beth in a frumpy dress. The hem was evened up and shortened a small amount. Notice how much longer her legs look. The first belt is too wide giving the waist too much weight and emphasis. The medium width belt is more in balance with the size of the plaid and total look.

Connie found a bargain – two dresses for the price of one. By adding a turtleneck and a leather belt to match her shoes, she created a completely different dress. The narrow sleeves can be worn pushed-up or long. With the buttons at front, no jewelry is needed. She could wear a scarf at the neckline, as on page 48 for another look.

WORKING WITH WHAT YOU'VE GOT

Unattractive

Attractive

Attractive

Unattractive

Beth likes the feel of the loose pleated shorts with slant pockets; but the legs are too wide. Notice the difference when the legs are tapered slightly: trim, sleek looking rather than too much fabric.

Again, a slight change in the side seam of the skort makes a world of difference. The first skort has a slight flair at the hemline, the second is straight. Too-long sleeves are uncomfortable and get in the way. When worn over a collar, scarves create a completely different neckline. With the addition of a vest on page 49, another look can be created.

64

WORKING WITH WHAT YOU'VE GOT

Unattractive

Attractive

Attractive

Unattractive

Dede loved this dress but never wore it. Now a blouse and skirt, it is a favorite. The blouse sleeves were set-in and tapered. The skirt was shortened and an elastic casing added. A belt was made from fabric from her altered suit – before suit on page 13, after on page 69. Isn't it exciting what can be done with some simple changes?

A classic blazer does not work for everyone, even if you love the fabric. Connie simply let out the side seams and darts in her blazer to give her the straighter look she needs. With the altered skort, she now has an attractive outfit.

SLEUTH SHOPPING

Now the fun part – sleuth shopping – seeking out, trying on, and admiring your new silhouette. For this trip, leave cash, checks, and credit cards at home. Go to stores where you would not normally shop. Be sure to wear your makeup and style your hair. You can wear comfortable shoes, but take along a dressy pair, the wrong shoe can ruin a good silhouette.

While sleuth shopping, let your imagination wander. Try on a variety of garments, even things you wouldn't buy or don't need. Get ideas. Take notes. Notice how fitting problems disappear with the correct silhouette.

Then go home and look in your closet. What do you absolutely need to add? What would you like to add? What can you afford to add?

BUYING THE RIGHT STUFF

Refer to your shopping notes and make a shopping list. Put a mark by what you need and a different mark by what you want. This list will grow and change over the months and years, but start with what's important now. Keep the list with you at all times. Watch for sales, shop at consignment stores, trade clothing with a friend, check catalogs. When you find that perfect something, **buy** it! It may appear impulsive but it's a planned purchase, you just didn't know when. Do **not** compromise! Buy exactly what you intended to.

During this time, you may want to start a portfolio of the new you silhouette. Look in mail order catalogs, pattern catalogs, magazines, and store ads. Clip pictures of clothing in your silhouette and make a scrapbook. This will help you add to your shopping list and keep your wardrobe updated.

THE END RESULTS

What you can expect from your efforts is a closet full of great looking styles that work for you. Whatever you grab will be **just** the right thing.

And, oh yes, be sure to smile and say, ''Thank you'' when you receive all those compliments!

''People who have style generally have a strong self-image and positive self-esteem – a strong sense of being.''
Way Bandy

MY VISION OF YOU

. . . a beautiful person, accepting and honoring the body shape you were born with, looking your best every day, exuding confidence, and receiving the admiration of your friends and peers . . .

Isn't it a wonderful feeling to know you can work with your body, just the way it is . . . **and** look terrific every day of your life? You don't have to wish you were different. What you have is special and gives you a unique look which is the real YOU!

Understanding your body shape and dressing in your silhouette is a major step in your personal growth and self awareness. If you follow the principles I've outlined in this book, I'm confident you'll agree the effort was well worth it. Ask someone who's tried it.

But I don't want to oversimplify dressing successfully. Your body shape determines the silhouette of your clothing. There are other factors which, together with body shape knowledge, help create a successful look. The colors you wear, your life style, profession, and personality all influence your clothing choices. If you haven't considered these aspects in determining your image, now might be a good time to pursue them.

I want you to have fun and enjoy working with the new you. Dressing harmoniously is not an overnight undertaking but a growing process. It can continue for as long as you want it to.

I truly believe, after more than 22 years of experience and working with thousands of people, that every one of us has the potential to develop our own style by dressing just right!

So go out there and be beautiful . . . you CAN do it.

. . . looking for the true, the good, and the beautiful
. . . and there you are.

68

© 1994 Darlene Miller

A LOT OF STYLE

NOTES

ORDER FORM

I would like to order additional copies of
Your Shape, Your Clothes & You

No. of copies _____ x $14.95 = _____

Shipping and handling:

   1st copy   x $3.00   = _____ $3.00 _____

   Additional copies:

   No. of copies_____ x $1.00   = _____

Total Cost of Order   = _____
(Enclose Check or Money Order)

Send order to:

     Clothes For You
     6 Rosebud Lane
     Missoula, MT 59801

NAME _____

ADDRESS _____

CIY _____ STATE ____ ZIP ____

PHONE _____

ORDER FORM

I would like to order additional copies of
Your Shape, Your Clothes & You

No. of copies_____ x $14.95 = _____

Shipping and handling:

   1st copy   x $3.00   = _____ $3.00 _____

   Additional copies:

   No. of copies_____ x $1.00   = _____

Total Cost of Order   = _____
(Enclose Check or Money Order)

Send order to:

     Clothes For You
     6 Rosebud Lane
     Missoula, MT 59801

NAME _____

ADDRESS _____

CIY _____ STATE ____ ZIP ____

PHONE _____

NOTES

NOTES